Exploring CUBA

THE OPENING OF CUBA, 2008-PRESENT

EXPLORING CUBA

Arts and Literature of Cuba

Cuba Under the Castros

Cuba: Facts and Figures

Cuban Music, Dance, and Celebrations

The Culture and People of Cuba

The Opening of Cuba, 2008-Present

Exploring CUBA

THE OPENING OF CUBA, ~~WITHDRAWN~~ 2008-PRESENT

John Ziff

MASON CREST
PHILADELPHIA

Mason Crest
450 Parkway Drive, Suite D
Broomall, PA 19008
www.masoncrest.com

Printed and bound in the United States of America.

CPSIA Compliance Information: Batch #EC2017.
For further information, contact Mason Crest at 1-866-MCP-Book.

First printing
1 3 5 7 9 8 6 4 2

Library of Congress Cataloging-in-Publication Data

on file at the Library of Congress
ISBN: 978-1-4222-3814-1 (hc)
ISBN: 978-1-4222-7981-6 (ebook)

EXPLORING CUBA series ISBN: 978-1-4222-3808-0

QR CODES AND LINKS TO THIRD-PARTY CONTENT

TABLE OF CONTENTS

1: Turbulent Times 7
2: Economic Reform:
    "Without Haste but Without Pause" 27
3: Repression in an Era of Reform 43
4: A New Era in U.S.-Cuba Relations 53
5: Limits of the Opening 65

Series Glossary of Key Terms......................................74
Further Reading 76
Internet Resources 77
Index 78
Photo Credits/About the Author...............................80

KEY ICONS TO LOOK FOR:

Words to understand: These words with their easy-to-understand definitions will increase the reader's understanding of the text while building vocabulary skills.

Sidebars: This boxed material within the main text allows readers to build knowledge, gain insights, explore possibilities, and broaden their perspectives by weaving together additional information to provide realistic and holistic perspectives.

Educational Videos: Readers can view videos by scanning our QR codes, providing them with additional educational content to supplement the text. Examples include news coverage, moments in history, speeches, iconic sports moments and much more!

Text-dependent questions: These questions send the reader back to the text for more careful attention to the evidence presented there.

Research projects: Readers are pointed toward areas of further inquiry connected to each chapter. Suggestions are provided for projects that encourage deeper research and analysis.

Series glossary of key terms: This back-of-the book glossary contains terminology used throughout this series. Words found here increase the reader's ability to read and comprehend higher-level books and articles in this field.

President Barack Obama (center) and First Lady Michelle Obama (right) stand in the rain shortly after their arrival in Havana, March 2016.

 WORDS TO UNDERSTAND IN THIS CHAPTER

collective farm—a farm, particularly in a communist country, that is controlled by the government and worked by many farmers.

executive order—in the United States, a presidential directive, issued to a part of the executive branch of government, that carries the force of law but can be overturned by a succeeding president.

nationalize—to transfer companies or entire industries from private to state ownership or control.

ration—a fixed amount of food or some other basic good officially allowed to each person during a time of shortage.

subsidize—to support another government, group, or individual financially, especially by paying part of the cost of something.

yanqui—in Latin American Spanish, a person from the United States.

TURBULENT TIMES

O n March 20, 2016—holding an umbrella to cover himself and his wife from a late afternoon drizzle— President Barack Obama descended the staircase of Air Force One and stepped onto the tarmac at José Martí International Airport in Havana. For Cubans, the scene would have seemed unimaginable just a couple years earlier. It wasn't simply that no American president had visited Cuba since 1928. More significantly, the island nation and its giant neighbor to the north had a history of antagonism dating back as far as most Cubans could remember.

For half a century, the U.S. government had tried to topple the Cuban regime, mostly through economic pressure but also, during the 1960s, by sponsoring an invasion of the island as well as multiple assassination attempts targeting Cuban dicta-

EDUCATIONAL VIDEO

To see a news report about President Obama's visit to Cuba, scan here:

tor Fidel Castro. For his part, Castro rarely missed an opportunity to castigate the United States—or to blame the *yanquis* for the many problems that beset Cuba under his leadership, particularly the island's chronically underperforming economy.

Failing health forced Fidel Castro to step down in 2008. Power passed to his brother Raúl, who gradually instituted a series of modest reforms. Those reforms concentrated on improving Cuba's economy. Raúl Castro gave little indication that his agenda included improved relations with the United States. However, in mid-2013 negotiators from the two countries began secret talks. And in December 2014 came the surprise announcement that Cuba and the United States would resume formal diplomatic relations, which had been severed in 1961. During the summer of 2015, Cuba opened an embassy in Washington, D.C., and the United States opened an embassy in Havana. All of this paved the way for President Obama's historic visit to Cuba.

Judging by the reception the president received, ordinary Cubans heartily approved of the thaw in relations with the United States. Throughout his three-day visit to the island, Obama was greeted by enthusiastic crowds. When he and his family toured San Cristóbal, Old Havana's 18th-century cathedral, onlookers erupted in a chant of "USA! USA!" Later, wav-

A sign on a Havana street welcomes Barack Obama to Cuba for his historic meeting with Raúl Castro, March 2016.

ing and cheering Cubans lined the route of the motorcade that took Obama to his first official meeting with Raúl Castro.

Among Cuba's ruling elite, the response to the American president's visit was considerably more muted. From the regime's perspective, greater engagement with the United States was a double-edged sword. On the one hand, Raúl Castro's efforts to reform Cuba's economy would be bolstered—indeed, had already been bolstered—by the loosening of American restrictions on travel to and commerce with the

Cubans cheer as President Obama's motorcade passes through Havana.

island. On the other hand, normalization of relations with the United States exposed Castro's regime to internal political pressures. No longer could the regime credibly lay its failures at Washington's door; it would instead have to own those failures. In addition, the loss of the United States as an enemy meant the loss of an important rationale the regime used to justify its authoritarian rule.

President Obama emphasized that point in a half-hour speech he delivered from Havana's historic Gran Teatro, or Grand Theater. "I believe my visit here demonstrates that you do not need to fear a threat from the United States," the president declared, addressing Raúl Castro directly. "And . . . I'm also confident that you need not fear the different voices of the Cuban people and their capacity to speak and assemble and vote for their leaders."

As Obama issued that challenge—and as he chided the Cuban regime at other points in his speech—Castro and his inner circle sat stone-faced. Ordinarily, Cubans don't see their leaders in an even mildly unflattering light, as the state maintains tight control over the media. But Obama's speech was broadcast live across the island.

In the days and weeks following Obama's visit, many Cuban officials lashed out at the American president. Foreign Minister Bruno Rodríguez, for example, blasted Obama's Cuba trip as "a deep attack on our political ideas, our history, our culture and our symbols."

But the questions remained: Where would Raúl Castro's reforms ultimately lead? Could the regime open up Cuba's economy, and embrace closer ties with the United States, while still maintaining its tight grip on political power? Or would Castro's reform program inevitably cause the upending of Cuba's repressive, one-party political system?

THE CUBAN REVOLUTION

Though independent since 1902, Cuba has had very little experience with democratic governance. Instead, dictatorships have been the rule.

Cuba's lone period of sustained and stable democracy, which began in 1940, ended just 12 years later. In 1952, Fulgencio Batista—the former chief of staff of the Cuban army—seized power in a coup and cancelled upcoming elections.

Initially, Batista enjoyed the support of the United States. He was extremely corrupt, skimming vast sums of money from the Cuban budget and even taking a cut of the profits generated by the American organized-crime families he permitted to operate in Havana. But Batista maintained a friendly climate for foreign businesses, and American corporations had large holdings in Cuba. These included sugar mills, cattle ranches, oil refineries, mines, banks, hotels, stores, and more.

Overall, Cuba was relatively prosperous. It had a sizeable middle class, in addition to an upper class consisting of business executives, large landowners, and the like. But hundreds of thousands of Cubans—mostly landless people in rural areas—lived in desperate poverty.

Batista's coup sparked a failed uprising in 1953. It was led by Fidel Castro, a lawyer by training. After serving a brief prison sentence, Castro planned another uprising, which began in December 1956. Castro and a small group of revolutionaries

Fulgencio Batista (center) shakes hands with Undersecretary of State Sumner Welles during the Cuban dictator's visit to Washington, D.C., in November 1938. U.S. officials had encouraged Batista to seize power, and they supported his government. Batista relinquished power in 1944 but launched a coup eight years later.

ensconced themselves in the Sierra Maestra, a rugged mountain range in eastern Cuba.

At first the rebels didn't seem to have much public support. But Batista ordered an increasingly vicious crackdown on his critics. Cubans who were merely suspected of opposing the regime faced arrest. Many were tortured or murdered by Batista's security forces. This brutality eventually alienated the

Cuban revolutionaries celebrate in the streets of Havana after their triumph over the Batista government, January 1, 1959.

majority of Cubans, and it caused the United States to cut off military aid to Batista's regime. By late 1958 Castro's revolutionaries had gained the upper hand, and on New Year's Day 1959, Batista fled the island.

BROKEN PROMISES

Castro had promised democracy, a free press, and respect for individual and political rights, and it's said that 9 in 10 Cubans supported his revolutionary government in 1959. Before too long, however, many Cubans began to grow wary of the new regime. The government shut down independent media. It harassed and imprisoned critics. Promised elections were never held. With the establishment, in 1960, of Committees for the Defense of the Revolution—neighborhood-level groups that monitored citizens for signs of disloyalty to the regime—Cuba was moving unmistakably toward a totalitarian system. The government demanded that citizens obey its dictates without question, and it sought to exert control over every aspect of people's lives.

Just months after coming to power, the Castro government took major actions affecting Cuba's economy. It seized property on the island belonging to IT&T, a huge American

Revolutionary leader Fidel Castro speaks to the media shortly after gaining power in Cuba, 1959.

telecommunications corporation. It also took large plantations, ranches, and farms, and outlawed land ownership by foreigners. Seized land was redistributed to landless Cuban peasants.

In 1960, the Castro government *nationalized* all U.S. companies and seized all American-owned property on the island. It also took over large and medium-sized Cuban businesses.

In response to the Castro government's repression, as well as its economic policies, almost a quarter million Cubans emigrated in the period 1959–1962. This was just the first of several major waves of emigrants who would leave Cuba over the years to escape the Castro regime. The majority went to the United States.

The Castro regime didn't allow Cuban citizens to leave the island at will. Rather, it was a crime, punishable by a prison sentence, to leave without the government's permission. An exit permit was required, and it cost too much for most Cubans to afford. Those who did have the means to obtain an exit permit knew they would still pay a steep price for deciding to emigrate. The government would confiscate their personal assets, and during the weeks or months it took for their paperwork to be processed, they would likely be subjected to official harassment. Would-be emigrants were fired from their jobs. Beginning in the mid-1960s, some were also made to toil in a labor camp before being allowed to leave Cuba.

OF CAPITALISM AND COMMUNISM

In February 1960, Castro's government concluded a trade agreement that would have enormous repercussions. Cuba's new trading partner would buy Cuban sugar, and in exchange Cuba would receive oil, grain, and financial credit. The terms of the deal were highly favorable to Cuba. But that's not what made the agreement so consequential. What made the agreement so consequential was that the other country involved was the Union of Soviet Socialist Republics (USSR).

Intentionally or not, Castro had drawn Cuba into a global conflict known as the Cold War. That conflict, which began in the late 1940s, pitted the USSR against the United States.

The United States and the USSR (also called the Soviet Union) were the world's most powerful countries. Each had a

Cuban leader Fidel Castro (left) speaks with Soviet premier Nikita S. Khrushchev during a meeting at the United Nations, 1960. The Castro government's ties to the communist Soviet Union led the United States to attempt to isolate Cuba through economic sanctions and travel restrictions.

massive arsenal of nuclear weapons, which, if they were ever used, might spell the end of civilization itself. Fortunately, the two superpowers avoided going to war directly with each other. However, they did support opposing sides in various civil wars and other conflicts around the world. Both superpowers also went to great lengths to enlist allies, and to prevent their adversary from bringing allies over to its side.

At the root of the Cold War lay two different political and economic systems—one espoused by the United States, and the other by the Soviet Union. Leaders in both countries believed that the two systems couldn't coexist peacefully in the long run.

The American political system was shaped by the ideals of liberal democracy. These include free, competitive elections. The U.S. economy, meanwhile, was undergirded by capitalism. To simplify a bit, capitalism is based on competition for profits by privately owned businesses.

According to communism—the ideology underpinning the Soviet Union's system—capitalism contains the seeds of its own destruction. Communist theory holds that capitalism will inevitably lead to the concentration of wealth in the hands of an ever-smaller class of business titans. These capitalists will exploit their workers, paying them miserably low wages. Eventually, though, the proletariat—the class of industrial workers (or, more broadly, all laborers)—will rise up and over-throw the capitalists.

After capitalism is swept away, according to communist theory, society must go through a stage of development known as socialism. During this stage, the state—acting in the interest of workers—controls the land, raw materials, factories, and machinery necessary for economic production. The state deter-mines how economic resources are allocated and which goods are produced. Though some inequality continues to exist, eco-nomic cooperation has replaced competition, as all workers have a stake in building a more prosperous society.

Eventually, society will pass into full communism. Communist theory paints an idyllic picture of this, the sup-posed final stage of historical development: Everyone's materi-

Memorial to Vladimir Lenin in Havana. Lenin (1870–1924) was a Russian revolutionary and communist. He founded the Bolshevik Party, which in October 1917 established the first government based on communist theories and principles. Lenin had a great influence on communist movements in other parts of the world, including Cuba.

al needs are fully met. Workers share common ownership of the things needed for economic production. The state itself becomes unnecessary and disappears.

Before the anticipated end of the state—while society is still at the socialist stage of development—communists usually insist that the Communist Party should be the only legal political party. They say it alone represents the interests of workers. Communists assert that liberal democracy is simply a tool for preserving capitalism.

ILL-ADVISED INVASION

As of 1960, Fidel Castro hadn't said that he subscribed to the tenets of communism. Nor had he characterized the Cuban Revolution as socialist in its goals. However, in the context of the Cold War, American policy makers found Cuba's February 1960 economic agreement with the Soviet Union alarming. The following month, President Dwight D. Eisenhower approved a secret plan to overthrow the Castro government.

The plan included restrictions on some U.S. trade with Cuba. But its most controversial element was a proposed invasion of the island by Cuban exiles who would receive equipment and training from the U.S. Central Intelligence Agency.

In early January 1961, during his final weeks in office, Eisenhower severed diplomatic relations with Cuba. But he left it up to his successor, John F. Kennedy, to decide whether to approve the invasion of Cuba. President Kennedy ultimately gave the operation a green light.

On April 17, 1961, some 1,400 Cuban exiles landed in southern Cuba at a place called the Bay of Pigs. But the exiles were unable to fight their way inland, and by April 19 the invasion had been crushed.

Castro soon declared Cuba a socialist country. By year's end, he'd admitted he was a full-fledged communist.

DREAMS OF FULL COMMUNISM

The failure of the Bay of Pigs invasion didn't end U.S. efforts to undermine the Castro regime. In early 1962, Kennedy issued an *executive order* targeting Cuba with a trade embargo. It not only banned all U.S. trade with Cuba (with the exception of

A Cuban fighter plane that defended the island against the 1961 Bay of Pigs invasion is preserved outside the Playa Giron Museum, which tells the story of the attack by Cuban exiles, who were secretly supported by the U.S. Central Intelligence Agency. The failed attempt to overthrow Castro's government contributed to poor relations between the United States and Cuba.

food and medicine) but also prohibited other countries that traded with Cuba from receiving U.S. foreign aid. A 1963 executive order forbade Americans to travel to the island, or to have any financial transactions with Cuba. Over the decades, U.S. sanctions against Cuba would be altered frequently—sometimes they were loosened, and sometimes tightened—but in one form or another the embargo remained in place. It took a big economic toll on Cuba.

Fortunately for the Castro government, the USSR was willing to generously *subsidize* the Cuban economy. The Soviets purchased Cuban sugar at well above the market price. They also sent more oil to Cuba than the island needed, enabling Cuba to export some.

By the mid-1960s, the socialist model was well entrenched in Cuba. All industry was under the control of the state. Agricultural production was organized around huge state-run *collective farms*. The state had taken ownership of businesses of any significant size. But Castro's government wasn't satisfied. "The aim of our revolution," a Cuban official noted in 1967, "is not to build a socialist state, but to move with minimum delay toward full Communism."

This sign in Baracoa reads: "With security and confidence we assume responsibility for the socialist future."

Castro railed against "idlers" who made money operating small businesses such as food stands, restaurants, bars, or handyman services. "If many are asking what kind of Revolution this is, that still permits such a class of parasites after nine years," he thundered in 1968, "they would be perfectly right to ask." The government soon "intervened" small businesses, bringing them, too, under state control and making private enterprise illegal. Now virtually every worker in Cuba was employed by the state.

Cuba's economy didn't thrive. The island faced chronic shortages of basic goods, and from 1963 on, the government issued its citizens monthly *ration* books for staples like rice, beans, and cooking oil. The Castro regime was certainly guilty of some extraordinary instances of economic mismanagement. But Cuba suffered from many of the same broad problems that plagued other communist countries. Central economic planning was inefficient and stifled innovation. Because workers were essentially guaranteed employment by the state, and because their salaries weren't linked to performance, incentives to work hard were relatively weak. Productivity suffered.

However, Soviet aid masked the actual scope of the problems afflicting Cuba's economy. The Cuban regime was thus insulated from some of the practical realities of Fidel Castro's vision of communism. But that changed abruptly three decades after the Cuban Revolution had brought Castro to power.

In an effort to focus on reforming his own country's system, Soviet leader Mikhail Gorbachev pulled back on the USSR's commitments to prop up other communist regimes. Beginning in 1989, the communist governments of Soviet-controlled Eastern Europe began to fall. Cuba saw its economic aid curtailed and then, after the Soviet Union broke apart in 1991, eliminated entirely.

"SPECIAL PERIOD"

The loss of Soviet subsidies plunged Cuba into a severe and prolonged economic crisis. Without a supply of oil, farm equipment couldn't be operated and electricity couldn't be generated to run factories. Cuban exports plummeted. So did imports, because Cuba had no way to pay for them. The result was widespread deprivation and hunger, which lasted for years.

The Cuban government called the crisis the "Special Period in Time of Peace," and Fidel Castro permitted some special—and un-communistic—policies to deal with it. State-owned collective farms were dismantled, with smaller agricultural cooperatives established in their place. To encourage the farmers who worked these cooperatives to produce more food, the government allowed them to sell a portion of their harvest for personal profit.

Notwithstanding Castro's earlier condemnation of small-business owners as "parasites," the government once again legalized self-employment in a limited number of fields. Those who wanted to work for themselves had to buy a license. The hiring of employees was prohibited, with the exception of operators of lunch stands and small restaurants, who were allowed to put family members on the payroll. The new policy was intended to help lower unemployment, which had skyrocketed with the closure of factories and other state-owned enterprises.

To obtain foreign exchange (currency from other countries), which Cuba desperately needed to pay for imported goods, the Castro regime made a major push to promote tourism. Cuba didn't have the facilities to accommodate large numbers of tourists, and it lacked the means to develop them quickly. So Castro was compelled to turn to the capitalist system he so despised. Deals were made with foreign, for-profit corporations to build and manage new hotels and resorts.

Once made, the decision to open the island to tourism couldn't readily be undone. But the economic reforms instituted during the Special Period could easily be reversed, and that's what Fidel Castro seemed poised to do after Cuba's economy had begun to recover.

 TEXT-DEPENDENT QUESTIONS

1. When did President Barack Obama visit Cuba? How long had it been since the last time a U.S. president visited the island?
2. Name the American president who approved the Bay of Pigs invasion.
3. What was the "Special Period"?

 RESEARCH PROJECT

In October 1962, Cuba was at the center of events that brought the United States and the Soviet Union to the brink of a nuclear war. Read about the Cuban Missile Crisis. Then write a brief report.

A Cuban man shops in a government store, where he can use his **libreta** (ration book) to purchase some food at heavily discounted prices. For more than fifty years, every Cuban family has been guaranteed a certain amount of rice, eggs, meat, bread, and other essentials. However, the government ration is often not enough, so Cubans must find other sources of food to survive.

 WORDS TO UNDERSTAND IN THIS CHAPTER

black market—trade in goods conducted in violation of laws or official regulations.

entrepreneur—a person who organizes, manages, and assumes the risk of a business.

means of production—physical factors (excluding human labor) that are used to produce goods, such as factories, machinery, tools, and raw materials.

private enterprise—a business that is owned and controlled by independent companies or private individuals rather than by the state; the system that fosters such businesses.

ECONOMIC REFORM: "WITHOUT HASTE BUT WITHOUT PAUSE"

Cuba had emerged from the Special Period by the turn of the 21st century. And its economy would get a huge boost from a deal reached in 2000 by Fidel Castro and Hugo Chávez, the socialist president of Venezuela. Under the agreement, oil-rich Venezuela would supply Cuba with petroleum. In return Cuba would send doctors, nurses, and other health care professionals to work in Venezuela. (Under Castro, Cuba had developed a first-rate health care system, and it had a large pool of well-trained doctors and nurses.) As had been the case with Cuba's earlier trade deals with the Soviet Union, the so-called oil-for-doctors agreement amounted to a large subsidy for the Cuban economy. The agreement effectively discounted the price of the oil. It also provided Cuba with more oil than the island needed domestically, enabling Cuba to re-export significant quantities.

ASSAILING THE ENTREPRENEURS

With Cuba's economic prospects brightening, the Castro government gave every indication that it intended to rein in self-employment and return the island to a purer form of socialism. Cuba had been obliged to permit some *private enterprise* during the Special Period, official sources said. However, Cuba's *cuentapropistas*, or self-employed *entrepreneurs*, were responsible for spreading such ills as "egotism, the cult of capitalist fetishes, and the mentality of the small property owner," according to the regime.

In 2004, the government issued new regulations covering private enterprise. For one-quarter of the previously allowed categories of self-employment, no new licenses would be issued, and existing licenses wouldn't be renewed. Lunch stands, cafeterias, and restaurants were among the private businesses that would be phased out in this manner. And after the new regulations took effect, the government began opening significant numbers of small state-run eating establishments.

The 2004 regulations left three-quarters of the self-employment categories—more than 115 specific lines of work—unaf-

EDUCATIONAL VIDEO

Scan here for a brief look at Cuba's changing economy:

During the late 1990s, Fidel Castro supported and encouraged a socialist politician from Venezuela named Hugo Chávez. The friendship paid off when Chávez gained power in Venezuela's government. In 2000 they made an agreement for Venezuela to ship 130,000 barrels of oil a day to Cuba at low prices—a huge boon to Cuba's economy.

fected. Though entrepreneurs in any of those categories could keep working, and could renew their licenses when those licenses expired, they still had reason for concern. The regulations stipulated that authorities would conduct reviews of the self-employment sector annually. And, at the government's discretion, any category of private enterprise could be "assimilated . . . by the central state administration."

In late 2005, Fidel Castro gave a blistering speech in which he assailed Cuba's self-employed "new rich" as betrayers of the

Cuban President Raúl Castro addresses the United Nations General Assembly in 2015. Raúl had been one of the key government leaders since the revolution, but had long been overshadowed by his older brother Fidel.

ideals of socialism. "The abuses will end," he declared ominously. "Many of the inequalities will disappear, as will the conditions that allowed them to exist."

NEW LEADER, NEW DIRECTION

In 2006, as he guided his country toward a retrenchment of socialism, Fidel Castro was stricken by a serious intestinal disease. Raúl Castro—who as first vice-president held Cuba's second most powerful position in government—became the provisional (temporary) president while his brother recovered. But in February 2008, still suffering from frail health, Fidel Castro officially resigned. Raúl Castro assumed the presidency on a regular basis.

"If we were to have two parties in Cuba," Raúl Castro observed, "Fidel would head one and I the other." The new president's approach to the economy was less ideological, and more flexible, than his brother's had been. Raúl was committed to socialism. But in his view socialism required only that the state maintain ownership of the fundamental *means of production*, not control the entire economy. And he was convinced that Cuba's socialist system wouldn't survive without changes. "We reform, or we sink," he told Cubans in a nationally broadcast speech.

Castro believed that in order to be successful, any reform effort would have to accomplish several critical goals. One was to reduce the number of people employed by the state and to make the state sector of the economy more efficient and profitable.

A second, related goal was to increase opportunities for entrepreneurship. An expanded private sector would help absorb workers laid off from downsized state-run enterprises. Plus, in Castro's view, entrepreneurs would spur greater economic output for the country as a whole. Of course, private enterprise would exist within an economy that remained primarily socialist. The state would retain control of the country's major industries and large enterprises. And many occupations, particularly in professional fields, would continue to be off-limits for those who wanted to go into business for themselves.

A third critical goal of Raúl Castro's economic reform agenda was less straightforward—and arguably more profound. Castro sought to modify the terms of the social contract his country's citizens had known for half a century, since the Cuban Revolution. The regime had always restricted citizens' political rights and personal freedoms, but Cubans who didn't challenge its authority understood that the government would meet their basic material needs. Housing was free. Health care was free. Employment was guaranteed, and so was a minimum amount of food. This didn't mean ordinary Cubans could expect to live comfortably. Far from it, in fact. Cramped and decrepit housing was common. Consumer goods that people in other countries took for granted were nonexistent in Cuba. And while the ration book entitled all Cubans to a monthly allotment of food and basic household necessities, it did not mean obtaining those goods wouldn't require standing in line for hours, or visiting multiple stores to find one that was actually stocked. Still, there was security in the knowledge that the government would provide citizens with the minimum necessary to get by.

Raúl Castro believed that too many Cubans had come to shirk personal responsibility, expecting the state to take care of them regardless of whether they showed any initiative or gave their full effort at their job. Castro aimed to end this "daddy state" attitude, as one top government official dubbed it, while still maintaining benefits considered vital to Cuba's socialist system, like free education and health care. "We have to erase forever the notion that Cuba is the only country in the world

A government ration store in Bayamo. The selection of merchandise available in these stores is often very limited. Cubans are used to going to different stores, and sometimes even different towns, in order to find even basic staples they need to survive.

where one can live without working," Castro told the National Assembly of People's Power, Cuba's legislature.

ROLLING OUT THE REFORMS

In 2010, after a period of analysis and debate among Cuba's government and Communist Party leaders, a major rollout of Raúl Castro's economic agenda began. In February, the government ended its long-standing policy of paying laid-off workers 60 percent of their salary. Then, in September, the government made a bombshell announcement: it intended to eliminate 500,000 state-sector jobs by mid-2011.

In some cases, affected workers might be offered positions in other state enterprises. But there were no guarantees, and the government made clear that it expected most laid-off state workers to find employment in the non-state, or private, sector. To facilitate that outcome, in October 2010 the government implemented new regulations covering private enterprise. A total of 181 lines of work—ranging from computer repair to

A vendor operates a stall in a street market in Trinidad. Small businesses must receive a government license to operate.

party clown—were opened up for new business licenses (that number would be expanded to 201 in 2014). In more than 80 of those lines of work, entrepreneurs would be allowed to hire employees (in 2016, the rules were changed to allow all licensed entrepreneurs to hire employees). This, the government hoped, would allow the private sector to evolve from one dominated by self-employment to one that accommodated small businesses.

Only about 140,000 state-sector jobs—less than 30 percent of the announced target of half a million—were eliminated in 2011. Nonetheless, the government declared that its ultimate goal was to shed at least a million state-sector jobs, and cuts continued—albeit at a rather measured pace—in the years that followed.

Raúl Castro insisted that there could be no turning back on the changes that had begun. And he promised that reforms would continue "without haste but without pause."

In 2011, the government made significant changes in agricultural policy. Farmers would now be permitted to lease unused land from the state. They'd be free to grow whatever they wanted. And, the government promised, they'd be able to sell their crops as they saw fit. For many independent farmers, Cuba's tourist sector offered excellent prospects for profit. Resort restaurants always needed fresh produce.

The leasing of government property also drove nonagricultural reforms. A pilot program launched in 2011 transferred state-owned barbershops and beauty salons to their employees. They rented their place of business from the government but operated as private collectives, with each worker having a share in the business. The former state employees were able to make their own rules, set their own prices, select their own company officers—and keep their profits.

The success of the pilot program led the government, beginning in 2012, to expand the private-cooperative model beyond barbershops and beauty salons. By January 2017, the Cuban government had registered 397 private, nonagricultural cooperatives.

Many of these cooperatives are cafeterias and restaurants. In 2014, the Cuban government announced its plans to get out of the dining business entirely—though with more than 9,000 state-run eating establishments across the island, that wouldn't happen overnight.

Private cooperatives also take some surprising forms. For example, a co-op called Taxi Rutero operates buses—the vehicles are leased from the government—along fixed routes in Havana. Its fares are much higher than those of the government bus system (23 cents versus 2 cents). But many riders use Taxi Rutero because it's more reliable than the notoriously erratic government bus system.

PERSISTENT CHALLENGES

Cuban society has changed dramatically—and probably irreversibly—with the opening of the island's economy to private enterprise. Gone is the assumption that the state will guarantee employment to its citizens for the duration of their working lives. A spirit of entrepreneurship flourishes—at least in some quarters.

Between 2008 and the end of 2016, state payrolls were

Tourists enter a tiny, privately owned restaurant in Trinidad. Small businesses like this are increasingly driving the Cuban economy.

FOR SALE: HOMES AND AUTOS

In 2011, the Cuban government passed a new property law that allowed Cuban citizens to buy and sell homes. Before, while every Cuban household technically owned the house or apartment in which they resided, the law forbade private transfers of real estate. No one could move without first applying for permission from the state, which, if permission was granted, would assign a new residence and fill the one vacated. No money changed hands.

The waiting period for moving could stretch to many months or even years, both because of the red tape involved and because of a shortage of available housing. This led to some difficult living arrangements—as, for example, when divorced couples found themselves forced to share a single-bedroom apartment for years. The government hoped the new law would help eliminate those sorts of situations, and to spur investment to improve and expand Cuba's housing stock.

Another 2011 law made it legal for Cuban citizens to buy and sell old cars. This primarily affected the 1950s-era American cars that are much in demand as taxis. The state maintained control of the sale of new vehicles.

reduced by more than 600,000 jobs. In 2015, according to official statistics, 24.3 percent of Cubans in the workforce—or nearly 1.2 million individuals—were employed in the non-state sector. This includes self-employed entrepreneurs, employees of entrepreneurs, private farmers, and workers in agricultural and nonagricultural collectives. It's estimated that the non-state sector grew to more than 27 percent in 2016. Just six years earlier, in 2010, it comprised only 16.2 percent of the active workforce, according to the Cuban government.

Foreign analysts suggest that the figures are probably somewhat inflated. Nonetheless, the trend is clear, and it is significant.

That's not to say the economic reforms spearheaded by Raúl Castro have been an unambiguous success. In some areas, they haven't even proceeded "without pause," as Castro pledged.

One major problem many entrepreneurs have faced is a lack of affordable supplies. The government still controls what is imported (as well as what is exported), and state-run enterprises are supplied before *cuentapropistas* have a chance to purchase what they need. And many businesses—such as *paladares*, or private restaurants—are legally required to buy their supplies from state-run stores, which are expensive. Buying goods on the *black market* can lead to a big fine, and possibly jail time. Some entrepreneurs resort to paying off government inspectors; corruption surrounding the private sector, as even the government acknowledges, is rampant. But enforcement of laws remains unpredictable. In late 2016, however, the Cuban government initiated a widespread crackdown on black-market purchases and other alleged violations by private restaurants, at the same time suspending the issuance of licenses for new *paladares*.

Private farmers also had reason to grumble in 2016. Because of a spike in food prices, the government reneged on its promise to permit independent farmers to market their own produce. Instead, it bought up the food, at low prices, for distribution at state-run markets. "They say we can't do as we please with our produce because there is not enough food," a vegetable farmer in western Cuba's Artemisa Province complained to a reporter. "Why is there not enough? Because there is nothing to work with! No fuel, no fertilizer, no pesticide, no nothing." Farmers still must rely on the government for these crucial inputs—as well as for seeds—and government inefficiencies have led to chronic shortages.

More fundamentally, the benefits of Cuba's economic reforms have been very uneven. Some of the most lucrative self-employment activities include running a snack bar, pizza shop, or *paladar*; renting rooms in one's home to tourists; and operating a private taxi. But getting started in these businesses requires resources to which most Cubans don't have access. Without a car, a person can't run a private taxi service. Cubans lucky enough to live in a decent neighborhood and have an extra room in their home still are likely to have to do costly renovations in order to accommodate tourists. And opening even a modest snack bar requires the equivalent of about $1,700—more than five and a half years of wages at the average state worker's 2015 salary of $25 per month.

Cubans receiving money from relatives living overseas have

disproportionately been able to take advantage of the most lucrative self-employment opportunities. For many others, self-employment means eking out a meager livelihood sewing clothes, repairing shoes, hawking trinkets to tourists, or engaging in some other marginal activity. And this has provoked considerable anger.

"[Government officials] sit there with a straight face," an engineer told Cuban independent journalist Iván García. "They blame the people for not working much and being used to living off the ration book. . . . Now they throw you out of work and tell you to start a business and figure it out for yourself. It's cynicism in its pure state."

 TEXT-DEPENDENT QUESTIONS

1. Why did Fidel Castro step down as Cuba's president?
2. What is a *cuentapropista*?
3. What are some common problems Cuban entrepreneurs face?

 RESEARCH PROJECT

Using the Internet, research the life of Raúl Castro. Write a one-page profile.

A bouquet of gladiolus flowers. The flowers have become a symbol of the Damas de Blanco protests in Havana.

 WORDS TO UNDERSTAND IN THIS CHAPTER

dissident—a person who strongly opposes and publicly criticizes a government, particularly an authoritarian one.

mercenary—a professional soldier hired to serve in a foreign army; a person who works or serves only for private gain and who is willing to set aside higher values such as ethics or patriotism.

political prisoner—a person imprisoned simply for criticizing a government or expressing political beliefs of which the government disapproves.

propaganda—information that is often false or exaggerated and that is spread in order to further a political cause.

sovereignty—freedom from external control; the authority of a state to govern itself.

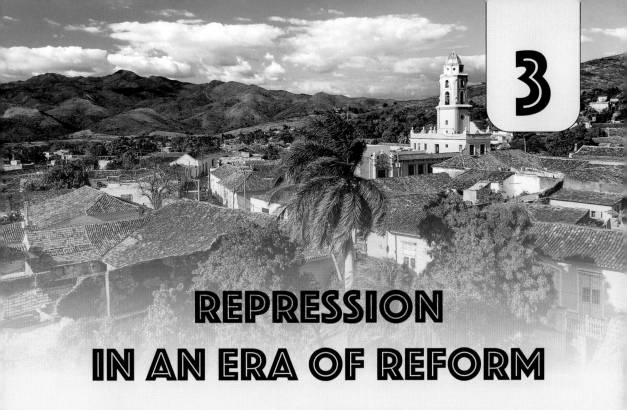

REPRESSION
IN AN ERA OF REFORM

Every Sunday, dozens of women dressed in white attend Mass together at a church in Havana. Around noon, when Mass is over, they begin a silent march along one of the capital city's major thoroughfares. Often the women carry a flower called a gladiolus, a traditional symbol of strength and integrity. Eventually they make their way to a park, where they assemble with a chant of *Libertad!* (Freedom!). They are known as the Damas de Blanco—the Ladies in White—and they've been following this weekly ritual, with slight variations, since 2003.

On some Sundays, the Ladies in White are accosted by mobs hissing insults and chanting pro-government slogans. Sometimes Cuban police and plainclothes state-security agents drag and shove the women into buses or vans, to be taken to

A Ladies in White demonstration in Havana, 2012.

police stations. That's because their weekly procession through the streets of Havana is a protest against the repression of the Cuban regime.

The Ladies in White formed during a period in Cuba that critics of the Castro government would come to call the "Black Spring." In March 2003, the Cuban regime rounded up 75 *dissidents*. They included human-rights activists, independent journalists and librarians, and advocates of democracy. Accused of being paid by the United States to undermine Cuban security or *sovereignty*, the dissidents were hastily tried and sentenced to prison terms of up to 28 years. To draw attention to the plight of these dissidents—all but one of whom was a man—their wives, mothers, sisters, and daughters formed the Ladies in White and began demonstrating on Sundays.

The Cuban government soon blasted the Ladies in White as "agitators" and "*mercenaries*" who were also in the employ of the *yanquis*. However, while it frequently subjected them to rough treatment, sometimes including beatings, and while it routinely arrested them, the government didn't imprison the Ladies in White. That probably had much to do with the international attention and support the group received. By 2005, the European Union had awarded the Ladies in White its highest honor for human-rights advocacy, the Sakharov Prize for Freedom of Thought.

EDUCATIONAL VIDEO

Scan here to see Cuban police break up a Ladies in White demonstration, 2016:

After Raúl Castro assumed Cuba's presidency, the dissidents swept up in the Black Spring crackdown were all released from prison. Most gained their freedom in 2010; the last two were released in March 2011.

But the Ladies in White didn't disband. They'd become one of Cuba's most recognized opposition groups, and they continued to demand that the government release all *political prisoners*, respect human rights, and permit citizens greater freedom.

FREEDOM TO TRAVEL

Cubans *have* seen some gains in personal—if not political—freedom since 2008. Of considerable significance is the ability to travel abroad. In January 2013, the Cuban government ended the requirement that citizens obtain an exit permit in order to leave the island legally. The government also extended, from 11 months to two years, the length of time Cuban citizens could remain abroad without losing residency—and thereby forfeiting their assets on the island, including their home.

The changes led to a surge of Cubans going overseas. Some, like Ladies in White leader Berta Soler and dissident blogger Yoani Sánchez, would never have been permitted to leave the island previously. They met with human-rights advocates and reporters, detailing the abuses of Cuba's government. Soler testified before the U.S. Congress.

Thousands of other Cubans went abroad to find jobs, knowing they'd merely have to visit their homeland once every two years to maintain residency. Tens of thousands of others didn't plan to return to Cuba at all, but instead sought to make their way to the United States. They knew that if they reached U.S. soil, even without a visa, they'd be able to stay in the United States and would be eligible for permanent resident status in one year. (President Obama ended this special treatment of Cuban undocumented migrants in January 2017.)

CELL PHONES AND COMPUTERS

The legalization of previously restricted information and communications technologies was another way Cubans' personal freedom expanded under Raúl Castro. Before 2008, only top Communist Party and government officials were allowed to have cell phones or computers. In May 2008, however, the gov-

The offerings are sparse at this state-run electronics and small-appliance store in Cienfuegos.

ernment began permitting ordinary Cubans to buy personal computers at state-run stores. And that August, Cubans were first allowed to sign up for mobile phone service, with the state-owned telecommunications monopoly.

The cost of a computer or a cell phone was beyond the means of many Cubans. In addition, Internet access—available to the general public only at government-run Internet cafés or, later, Wi-Fi hotspots—was also expensive. As of 2015, it was estimated that only 30 percent of Cubans had a cell phone, and only slightly more (31 percent) had Internet access. Still, with several million people having access to text messaging, email, social media, and the websites of foreign newspapers such as the *Miami Herald* and the *New York Times*, the flow of information in Cuba has become considerably freer.

Until late 2016, home Internet access was illegal for ordinary Cubans (the few exceptions included doctors, professors, and journalists employed by the state). That changed with a small pilot program that brought the Internet into 2,000 homes in Havana. The government set a goal of delivering broadband Internet service to half of Cuban households by 2020.

THE SUPPRESSION OF DISSENT

That goal of dramatically increasing Internet access could produce additional headaches for a regime intent on political censorship. The government routinely blocks independent news sites produced by Cubans, as well as blogs that offer "counter-revolutionary" criticism of political conditions on the island. In some cases, however, the producers of these websites email them to friends overseas, who ensure they are posted. This enables Cuban exiles (and other interested people) to read them. Even on the island, Cubans have found ways to thwart online censorship. For example, some dissident websites are copied onto flash drives, which are clandestinely passed from person to person to be downloaded.

If preventing the digital spread of "counterrevolutionary" content has proved problematic, the Cuban government maintains an iron grip on print and broadcast news media. All newspapers published on the island are controlled by the state.

Cubans are constantly bombarded with pro-regime messages. The facade of this building in Santiago de Cuba exhorts everyone to greater effort for the revolution and declares, "We will overcome!" The regime's agenda is also promoted through propaganda in the news media, which is tightly controlled by the government.

So, also, are Cuba's handful of radio stations and its two television networks. Government *propaganda* is a staple of these outlets. A free press does not exist in Cuba. That's underscored in the annual reports issued by Freedom House, a Washington, D.C.–based nongovernmental organization that monitors political rights and civil liberties around the globe. In the organization's 2016 analysis, only 5 of 202 countries and territories had less freedom of the press than Cuba.

Similarly, international human-rights organizations such as Human Rights Watch (which is headquartered in New York City) and Amnesty International (headquartered in London) have harshly criticized the Cuban government's overall record on human rights. In the past, the regime used large-scale incarceration as a primary means of stifling dissent. During the late 1960s, for example, Fidel Castro acknowledged that Cuba had 20,000 political prisoners—and independent experts estimated the actual number at 40,000 or more. As of 2016, according to most human-rights groups, the number of political prisoners on the island was probably between four or five dozen and a couple hundred.

Under Raúl Castro, arbitrary arrest and short-term detention are among the favored methods of dealing with dissidents. Many critics of the government find themselves taken into custody, without charge, by the police or state-security agents. They may be held for a few hours or a couple days before being released. And this happens repeatedly.

Dissidents also sometimes face what the regime calls "acts of repudiation." These are essentially government-directed mob actions in which the target is publicly intimidated or humiliated through threats, verbal abuse, or physical assault.

Cuba may have opened up economically under Raúl Castro. But, like his brother, he showed little inclination to relax political repression. Cuba has remained a communist dictatorship.

 TEXT-DEPENDENT QUESTIONS

1. What initially led the Ladies in White to organize their protests?
2. In what ways has the Cuban government permitted citizens greater personal freedom since 2008?
3. How many political prisoners did Fidel Castro say Cuba had in the late 1960s?

 RESEARCH PROJECT

Pick 10 countries, making sure each of the six inhabited continents is represented by at least one country. How free do you think each country's news media is? Place each country into one of these categories: Free, Partly Free, or Not Free. Now go to the site

https://freedomhouse.org/reports

and check your guesses against Freedom House's "Freedom of the Press" ratings.

Pedestrians walk past a sign welcoming Barack Obama to Cuba, 2016.

 WORDS TO UNDERSTAND IN THIS CHAPTER

bilateral—involving two countries.

expeditious—marked by prompt efficiency; speedy.

overture—an initiative toward agreement or action.

subversive—intended to or having the effect of undermining or destroying an established government.

A NEW ERA
IN CUBA-U.S. RELATIONS

In 2008, when Raúl Castro was elevated from acting president to regular president, relations between Cuba and the United States were at a low point. And there seemed little reason to expect anything other than a continuation of the long-running antagonism between the two countries.

U.S. president George W. Bush, elected in 2000 and reelected in 2004, had adopted a confrontational stance toward the Castro regime. He'd very publicly announced the creation of a high-level commission, co-chaired by Secretary of State Colin Powell, whose stated mission was to develop a plan to help bring about "an *expeditious* end of the [Castro] dictatorship." In an October 2007 speech that was broadcast to the island by Radio Martí—a Miami-based station funded by the U.S. government—Bush suggested that the Cuban people were on the

This mural on a wall in Havana, painted in 2005, depicts U.S. president George W. Bush as a warmonger playing a game with Death, using weapons as chess pieces.

cusp of rebelling against the regime. He addressed members of Cuba's government, armed forces, and police directly. "When Cubans rise up to demand their liberty, the liberty they deserve, you've got to make a choice," he said. "Will you defend a disgraced and dying order by using force against your own people, or will you embrace your people's desire for change?"

Needless to say, the Cuban regime was none too happy with those comments, or with the Bush administration's policy generally. In a February 2008 speech before the National Assembly of People's Power, Raúl Castro characterized American policy as a "real war waged by the United States administration" against Cuba. "Their intention," he said, "has not changed from the triumph of the Revolution, [that is,] to make our people suffer as much as possible in order to force it to abandon its decision to be free."

CHANGING COURSE

During his 2008 presidential campaign, Barack Obama called for a fresh approach to the issue of U.S.-Cuba relations. "We've been engaged in a failed policy with Cuba for the last 50 years," he asserted. "And we need to change it."

Instead of isolating Cuba, Obama favored U.S. engagement with the Castro government on issues of mutual interest—though he said the U.S. trade embargo should remain in place until Cuba made moves to democratize. Obama also pledged that, if elected, he would remove restrictions on Cuban-Americans' freedom to visit and help relatives on the island financially.

Barack Obama, of course, was elected president. And in April 2009, three months after taking the oath of office, he fulfilled one of his campaign promises regarding Cuba. He did away with Bush administration rules under which Cuban-Americans had been permitted to visit the island just once every three years, and to send a

EDUCATIONAL VIDEO

Scan here to watch a brief history of U.S.-Cuba relations:

President Obama talks on the phone with Raúl Castro while a group of his advisors waits in the Oval Office, December 16, 2014. The next day, the president announced that the United States would restore full relations with Cuba after more than 50 years.

maximum of $300 to their relatives every three months. Now there would be no limits on how often Cuban-Americans could visit the island, and no cap on the cash remittances they could send relatives. The resulting flow of dollars would give many of Cuba's new entrepreneurs their start in business.

In June 2009, the Obama administration made another gesture designed to foster engagement with Cuba. At the 39th General Assembly of the Organization of American States, which convened in Honduras, the U.S. delegation promoted a resolution to restore Cuba's OAS membership. Cuba had been expelled from the OAS, an association of Western Hemisphere countries, in 1962, at the insistence of the United States. The 2009 resolution was approved, though Cuba ultimately declined to rejoin the OAS, citing past grievances with the organization.

Still, the U.S. *overture* didn't go unnoticed. And, as candidate Barack Obama had suggested, the two countries began discussions on issues of mutual interest, such as migration and the restoration of direct mail service. Though these steps were small, the thaw in U.S.-Cuba relations was apparent. By year's end, however, progress in the *bilateral* relationship had come to a screeching halt.

A SETBACK AND A BREAKTHROUGH

In early December 2009, Cuban authorities arrested an American named Alan P. Gross. A contractor for the U.S. Agency for International Development (USAID), Gross had been employed for a "democracy promotion" program. He'd distributed computers and satellites to, and set up Wi-Fi hotspots for, Jewish community groups on the island. In March 2011, a Cuban court convicted him of "acts against the independence and territorial integrity of the state." He was sentenced to 15 years in prison.

The incident provoked heated recriminations from both sides. "It is appalling," an American spokesperson said, "that the Cuban government seeks to criminalize what most of the world deems normal, in this case access to information and technology." For its part, the Cuban government condemned Gross's activities as "a *subversive* project of the U.S. government that aimed to destroy the revolution through the use of communications systems out of the government control."

Engagement with Cuba was shelved for the remainder of Obama's first term. Shortly after he won reelection in November 2012, however, the president approved another approach. A message passed to the Castro regime signaled the willingness of the White House to have a dialogue—provided the issues were confined to counterterrorism and a possible prisoner exchange, and provided the discussions were conducted in the strictest secrecy. The Castro regime agreed to the terms.

A small group—three Americans and four Cubans—first met in June 2013 in Ottawa, Canada. It was understood that both delegations spoke for their respective presidents. The initial meeting produced no agreement, but the delegations periodically returned to Ottawa throughout the summer and fall. Late in the year, the Americans broadened the scope of the discussions. "We decided to put everything on the table," recalled Ben Rhodes, one of the three American negotiators. "Normalization, diplomatic relations, regulatory changes."

The Cubans hesitated, and for months the discussions remained stalled. A breakthrough came after Pope Francis sent personal letters to Raúl Castro and Barack Obama, appealing for them to work through their differences and offering the Vatican's assistance as a mediator. The intervention of the Argentina-born pope—the first head of the Roman Catholic Church from the Western Hemisphere—apparently convinced the wavering Castro to move forward.

Just after noon on December 17, 2014, Castro and Obama

Alan Gross walks on the tarmac at an airport near Havana shortly after his release from a Cuban prison, December 17, 2014. He is accompanied by his wife Judy, as well as Senator Patrick Leahy (D-VT), Congressman Chris Van Hollen (D-MD), and Senator Jeff Flake (R-AZ). Gross spent five years in a Cuban prison as an accused spy, and was released as part of a U.S. and Cuban government effort to improve relations.

appeared simultaneously on live TV in their respective countries. The two presidents made the stunning announcement that Cuba and the United States had agreed to normalize relations.

Prisoner releases accompanied the announcements. Cuba freed Alan Gross and a Cuban intelligence officer who'd spied for the United States, as well as 53 political prisoners. The United States released three Cuban intelligence agents who'd been arrested in Miami in 1998.

COMMERCE

Following the announcement of normalized relations, President Obama set about relaxing U.S. restrictions on commerce with Cuba. Though a full repeal of the economic embargo would require an act of Congress, the president had considerable latitude to ease financial, trade, and travel constraints through the use of executive orders.

As a result of the executive orders, American companies in certain industries—including telecommunications, travel, hospitality, and banking—were now legally permitted to conduct business in Cuba. Of course, they'd first have to negotiate deals with the Cuban government, which many sources have described as an unpredictable and often frustrating process. Still, the Cuban government approved some major business deals with American companies. For example, Sprint and Verizon won approval to offer wireless roaming telephone and data service on the island, in partnership with Cuba's state-run telecommunications company. Google won approval to put servers in Cuba and to expand broadband Internet access there. Starwood Hotels & Resorts signed a deal to manage several hotels in Havana.

Obama executive orders also paved the way for direct commercial flights from the United States to Cuba. Ten U.S. carriers were flying to Cuba by 2017. In addition, several American cruise lines, including Miami-based Carnival, began calling in Cuba.

The airlines and cruise ships served a rising tide of American visitors to the island. All told, Cuba recorded more than 405,000 visits by travelers from the United States, includ-

Tourists disembark from a cruise ship docked at Havana.

ing Cuban-Americans, in 2015. By 2016 that figure had risen to close to 615,000. Technically, it remained illegal under the embargo for Americans to visit Cuba purely for the purpose of tourism. But regulations put in place by the Obama administration defined a dozen categories of permissible travel, and many visitors could qualify under one of those categories.

DISCONTENTS

Not everyone was happy with the changes in Cuba-U.S. relations set in motion by Barack Obama and Raúl Castro. And that was true on both sides of the Florida Strait. Obama critics slammed the president for allowing the Cuban government to reap the economic benefits of increased commerce with the United States without improving its human-rights record or taking steps toward democratization. "The Castro regime," railed Senator Marco Rubio of Florida, the child of a Cuban exile, "has made out like bandits and received numerous concessions from the U.S. without lifting a finger to . . . allow the Cuban people to exercise their God-given freedoms."

Senator Ted Cruz, a Republican from Texas, is the son of a Cuban exile. Like many Cuban-Americans, he was critical of the Obama administration's attempt to improve relations with Cuba.

In Cuba some hard-liners continued to insist that increased commercial ties with the United States could only corrupt Cuba's socialist system, thereby destroying the accomplishments of the revolution. Some even suggested that was the *yanquis*' real goal in engaging Cuba. One such hard-liner was Raúl Castro's brother. In a scathing letter published in the Communist Party newspaper *Granma* shortly after Barack Obama's March 2016 visit, Fidel Castro mocked the president's call for Cuba and the United States to leave the past behind and look toward a hopeful future. "I suppose all of us were at risk of a heart attack upon hearing [those] words," Castro wrote.

> Nobody should be under the illusion that the people of this dignified and selfless country will renounce the glory, the rights, or the spiritual wealth they have gained with the development of education, science and culture.
>
> .... We are capable of producing the food and material riches we need with the efforts and intelligence of our people. We do not need the empire [the United States] to give us anything.

 TEXT-DEPENDENT QUESTIONS

1. Who said: "We've been engaged in a failed policy with Cuba for the last 50 years. And we need to change it"?
2. What is the name of the USAID contractor whose 2009 arrest sidetracked U.S.-Cuba engagement?
3. When was the announcement of the normalization of U.S.-Cuba relations made? By whom?

 RESEARCH PROJECT

The Cuban intelligence agents freed when normalization of U.S.-Cuba relations was announced were part of a spy ring known in the United States as the "Cuban Five" or the "Miami Five." In Cuba they were dubbed the "Five Heroes." Research the case. What was their mission in Miami? How were they caught? Present your findings in a short report.

President Obama's car drives past the Ministry of the Interior building in Havana, which includes a giant sculpture depicting revolutionary hero Che Guevara with the slogan "Hasta la Victoria Siempre" ("Towards Victory Forever"). Though U.S.-Cuba relations have improved, it is uncertain how long the thaw will last.

 WORDS TO UNDERSTAND IN THIS CHAPTER

fervor—intense and passionate feeling; zeal.

gross domestic product (GDP)—the total value of goods and services produced in a country in a one-year period.

LIMITS OF THE OPENING

The opening of Cuba is ongoing. And it's impossible to predict where, precisely, the changes introduced since 2008 will lead. What will the country look like in a decade's time? Will the state and non-state sectors of the economy reach an equilibrium that makes possible the attainment of a "sustainable and prosperous model of socialism," Raúl Castro's stated goal? If so, will prosperity increase or lessen pressures for political reform? As Cuba's revolutionary generation passes from the scene, how will a younger generation of Communist Party leaders govern? How might U.S. relations with Cuba evolve?

EXIT, FIDEL

By any measure, 2016 was a consequential year for Cuba. Certainly the most publicized development was the death, on

Cuban mourners wave flags as the remains of Fidel Castro pass through the streets of Sancti Spíritus in a parade, December 1, 2016.

Cuban-Americans celebrate the news of Castro's death, November 26, 2016.

November 25, of Fidel Castro. The revolutionary leader was 90. Though he'd had no formal role in government for eight years, Castro had continued to make his opinions known, through articles and letters in state publications, until his final months. At best he was skeptical of the course charted by his brother. Sometimes he seemed barely able to contain his exasperation.

EDUCATIONAL VIDEO

Scan here to see reactions to the death of Fidel Castro in Havana and Miami:

In retirement, some Cuba analysts suggest, Fidel had acted as a brake on Raúl's reform agenda. His stature ensured that, even if Raúl couldn't be dissuaded from opening up the country in various ways, he would at least tread cautiously in doing so. Certain lines wouldn't be crossed. In this view, Fidel Castro's death would pave the way for more aggressive implementation of reforms. "Now that Fidel is gone," noted Joel Ross, a Latin America analyst based in Britain, "there may be a boldening, a quickening of the economic reforms. . . . There may be a louder voice . . . from the side of the reformers, the modernizers to allow more economic progress."

Other observers attribute the tentative pace of reforms from 2008 to 2016 not to deference toward Fidel, but to Raúl's own determination to avoid upsetting the order established by the Cuban Revolution. "The thing about Raúl," observed William Rowlandson, a senior lecturer in Hispanic Studies at the University of Kent, "is he's still very much tied to the past."

President Obama shakes hands with Raúl Castro during the Summit of the Americas in Panama, April 11, 2015. This handshake marked the culmination of years of talks between the Obama administration and the Castro government.

In any case, Raúl didn't have too much time to implement bolder reforms after Fidel's death, presuming he was so inclined. He'd pledged to step down as president in February 2018.

A SPUTTERING ECONOMY

Economically, 2016 was a bad year for Cuba. The government had projected *gross domestic product (GDP)* to grow at a modest rate of 2.0 percent. Instead, GDP declined by 0.9 percent from 2015, according to official government figures.

Much of the downturn could be attributed to an economic and political crisis in Venezuela. As a result of that crisis,

Venezuela slashed its oil shipments to Cuba, which were heavily subsidized under the 2000 "oil-for-doctors" agreement.

Though Venezuela's problems had been brewing for a while, Cuba's economic planners were caught flat-footed. "It was clear the Venezuelan crisis at some point would have a negative impact on the Cuban economy," noted economist Pavel Vidal. "Nevertheless, the commercial and financial dependence on Venezuela remained high and not enough was done to search for alternatives."

One alternative would have been to try to attract more foreign investment by relaxing rules that effectively limit foreign ownership stakes in enterprises on the island to 50 percent. Another alternative would have been to accelerate approval of deals with American companies.

What would help Cuba's economy even more would be a lifting of the U.S. trade embargo. One recent study estimated

 PUBLIC OPINION AND THE EMBARGO

Most Americans support getting rid of trade sanctions against Cuba. A December 2016 survey by the Pew Research Center found nearly three in four Americans (73 percent) favored ending the embargo. Attitudes have shifted even in the Cuban-American community, which was once overwhelmingly opposed to any accommodation with the Castro regime. Sixty-three percent of Cuban-Americans in Miami-Dade County (home to the country's largest Cuban-American community) opposed the embargo in a poll conducted by Florida International University from July to August 2016.

President Donald J. Trump addresses the crowd at a rally in Louisville, Kentucky, March 2017. During his campaign, Trump threatened to close the U.S. embassy in Havana if the Cuban government did not meet his demands for "religious and political freedom for the Cuban people and the freeing of political prisoners."

that Cuba would export $5.8 billion worth of goods annually to the United States if the embargo ended.

CANCEL THE "DEAL"?

With certain key members of Congress vehemently opposed to any action that might help Cuba's communist regime, few observers expected an end to the embargo in the near future. But the 2016 presidential election cast doubt on the entire direction of U.S.-Cuba relations.

Hillary Clinton, the Democratic Party's presidential nominee, had served as secretary of state in the Obama administration. And if elected, she said, she would continue Obama's efforts to open Cuba to as much U.S. commerce and people-to-people contact as was possible while the embargo remained in effect. Ultimately, she would press to have the embargo repealed. However, Clinton was defeated in the 2016 general election by the Republican Party's candidate, businessman Donald Trump.

Trump had harshly criticized the Obama administration's Cuba policy—though he was a bit vague about details. "We will cancel Obama's one-sided Cuban deal, made by executive order," he said, "if we do not get the deal that we want and the deal that people living in Cuba and here deserve, including protecting religious and political freedom."

If he chose, President Trump could use executive orders to roll back virtually every opening to Cuba his predecessor had made: on commerce, on travel, even on normalization of diplomatic relations. Some U.S. businesses would pay a price, and that could well temper the Trump administration's zeal for turning back the calendar to 2009. Still, many Cubans have told reporters they're worried.

RAÚL'S WAGER

We reform, or we sink. That's the stark choice Raúl Castro laid out for the Cuban people. But it wasn't really the Cuban people that were at risk of going under in the absence of reform. It was the socialist system birthed by the Cuban Revolution. It was the one-party state.

More than six decades of communist rule have sapped much of the revolutionary *fervor* of the Cuban people. That's attested to by foreign journalists and scholars who have visited the island. It's also borne out by a rare opinion poll conducted in Cuba without the government's authorization or knowledge. The survey, conducted in 2015 on behalf of the U.S. Spanish-language broadcaster Univision, found that just 39 percent of Cubans were satisfied with their country's political system, compared with 53 percent who were dissatisfied. Close to six in 10 (58 percent) rated the Communist Party negatively, and just one in three (32 percent) positively.

In the past, the regime was able to use the threat posed by the *yanqui* enemy to rally the Cuban people. But in the Univision poll, a majority of Cubans said the United States was now a friend to their country, and nearly everyone believed normalization of relations was good for Cuba.

Pressures for political change on the island are simmering. In the Univision poll, only 28 percent said they were satisfied with Cuba's one-party system; 52 percent believed the country should have more political parties. As far as the regime is concerned, though, that idea is off the table. At the Communist Party's 2016 congress, Raúl Castro described the call for free, multiparty elections as a ruse to destroy Cuba. "If they manage some day to fragment us," he said, "it would be the beginning of the end . . . of the revolution, socialism and national independence."

In embarking on his reform agenda, Raúl Castro was essentially wagering that a more open economy, and a somewhat more open society, wouldn't be incompatible with a closed, authoritarian political system. Better material circumstances would satisfy most people, and continued repression would muzzle the rest, enabling the Communist Party to maintain its monopoly on power. It remains to be seen whether that formula will work in the long run.

 TEXT-DEPENDENT QUESTIONS

1. What significant event happened in Cuba on November 25, 2016?
2. What external development helped make 2016 a bad year for Cuba's economy?
3. Who threatened to "cancel Obama's one-sided Cuban deal"?

 RESEARCH PROJECT

Make a timeline of developments in Cuba from 2008 to the present.

Series Glossary

asylee—in the United States, an alien who receives asylum, meeting the legal definition of an individual who is unable or unwilling to return to his or her home country due to a fear of persecution on account of race, religion, nationality, political opinion, or membership in a particular social group.

asylum—protection granted by a government to a refugee from another country.

authoritarian—favoring blind submission to authority.

capitalism—an economic system that permits the ownership of private property, allows individuals and companies to compete for their own economic gain, and generally lets free market forces determine the price of goods and services.

communism—a political and economic system that champions the elimination of private property and common ownership of goods, for the benefit of all members of society.

deportation—the formal removal of an alien after he or she has broken immigration laws.

ideology—a systematic set of principles and goals.

indoctrination—instruction in the basic principles of a political party or other organization.

lobby—an organized attempt to convince a legislator to vote a certain way on an issue.

nationalism—a sense of national consciousness; promotion of the interests of one's own nation above the interests of other nations.

paramilitary—relating to a force organized along military lines but not composed of official soldiers.

proletariat—the class of industrial workers.

refugee—a person who is unable or unwilling to return to his or her country of nationality because of persecution or a well-founded fear of persecution.

socialism—an economic system that is based on cooperation rather than competition and that utilizes centralized planning and distribution, controlled by the government; in Marxist theory, an intermediate stage between capitalism and communism during which the state—controlled by the proletariat—owns all factories and other places of work, and wages and the distribution of goods are still somewhat unequal.

totalitarian—relating to a political regime that seeks to exert complete control over citizens' lives.

Further Reading

Cooke, Julia. *The Other Side of Paradise: Life in the New Cuba*. Berkeley, CA: Seal Press, 2014.

Feinberg, Richard E. *Open for Business: Building The New Cuban Economy*. Washington, DC: Brookings Institution Press, 2016.

Mesa-Lago, Carmelo, and Jorge Pérez-López. *Cuba Under Raúl Castro: Assessing the Reforms*. Boulder, CO: Lynne Rienner Publishers, 2013.

Pérez, Louis A., Jr. *Cuba: Between Reform and Revolution*. 5th ed. New York: Oxford University Press, 2015.

Sánchez, Yoani, and M. J. Porter (translator). *Havana Real: One Woman Fights to Tell the Truth About Cuba Today*. Brooklyn, NY: Melville House Publishing, 2011.

Internet Resources

www.youtube.com/watch?v=xbzvOaseef4
    David Muir of ABC News conducted this interview
    with Barack Obama during the president's historic
    2016 trip to Cuba.

www.brookings.edu/topic/cuba/
    Reports on various aspects of Cuba today—including
    the economy, social conditions, and relations with the
    United States—from the Brookings Institution, a think
    tank based in Washington, D.C.

www.cia.gov/library/publications/the-world-
    factbook/geos/cu.html
    The CIA World Factbook's Cuba page contains basic
    information about the island's geography, government,
    people and society, economy, and more.

www.14ymedio.com/englishedition
    The English-language edition of *14ymedio*, an inde-
    pendent online publication cofounded by Yoani
    Sánchez, a pioneering Cuban blogger, and Reinaldo
    Escobar, a Cuban journalist.

Index

"acts of repudiation," 50–51
agricultural policy, 35, 40
    and collective farms, 6, 22, 24
    See also economy, Cuban
Amnesty International, 50
assassination attempts, U.S., 7–8

Batista, Fulgencio, 12, 13–14
Bay of Pigs invasion, 7, 20, *21*
black market, 26, 39–40
"Black Spring," 44–45
Bush, George W., 53–55

capitalism, 18, 19, 25
    See also communism
car sales, 38
Castro, Fidel, *15, 17*
    assassination attempts on, 7–8
    and the Cold War, 16–17, 20
    and the Cuban Revolution, 12–13, 14–15, 20
    death of, 65, *66*, 67–68
    and dissidents, 44–45, 50
    and the economy, 15, 16, 20–25, 27, 28–30
    and emigration, 16
    and normalization of U.S.-Cuba relations,
      62–63, 67
    resignation of, 8, 31
    and small businesses, 23, 24, 28–30
    and the "Special Period," 24–25, 27
Castro, Raúl, *30, 68*
    as acting president, 30–31, 53
    and "acts of repudiation," 50–51
    and the Bush administration, 54–55
    and dissidents, 45, 50–51
    and economic reform, 8, 9, 11–12, 30–36, 38,

      39–41, 67, 69, 71, 72–73
    and human rights, 45–48, 50–51
    and normalization of U.S.-Cuba relations, 8–9,
      11–12, *56*, 58–60, 61–63, 65, 67, 72–73
    and Barack Obama's visit (2016), 7, 8–9, 11–12
    and private enterprise restrictions, 39–41
    and resignation of presidency, 68
cell phones, 46–48, 60
censorship, 48, 50
Central Intelligence Agency (CIA), 20, *21*
Chávez, Hugo, 27, *29*
Clinton, Hillary, 71
Cold War, 16–21
collective farms, 6, 22, 24
    See also agricultural policy
Committees for the Defense of the Revolution, 15
communism, 18–20, 23–24
    in Cuba, 22–23, 24, 33–34, 46, 51, 62, 65, 72–73
Communist Party, 19, 33–34, 46, 62, 65, 72–73
computers, 47–48, 57
corporations, American, 12, 15, 60, 69
Cruz, Ted, 62
Cuba
    "acts of repudiation" in, 50–51
    "Black Spring" in, 44–45
    censorship in, 48, 50
    and the Cuban Revolution, 12–13, 14–15, 20
    democracy in, 12
    dissidents in, 43–45, 46, 50–51
    economy of, 8, 9, 11–12, 15, 16, 20–25, 27–36,
      38, 39–41, 60–61, 67, 68–69, 71–73
    emigration from, 15–16, 46
    gross domestic product (GDP) of, 68
    health care system in, 27
    human rights in, 43–48, 50–51

Numbers in **bold italic** refer to captions.

Jewish community groups in, 57
and normalization of U.S.-Cuba relations, 8–9,
11–12, *56*, 58–63, 67, 72–73
and the Organization of American States
(OAS), 56–57
and private enterprise restrictions, 39–41
protests in, 43–45
and the "Special Period," 24–25, 27
Cuban Revolution, 12–13, 14–15, 20
cuentapropistas (self-employed), 28, 39
See also private enterprise

Damas de Blanco. *See* Ladies in White (Damas de
Blanco)
diplomatic relations. *See* U.S.-Cuba relations
dissidents, 43–45, 46, 50–51
and political prisoners, 42, 44–45, 50, 59

economy, Cuban
and agricultural policy, 6, 22, 24, 35, 40
and the black market, 39–40
under Fidel Castro, 15, 16, 20–25
under Raúl Castro, 8, 9, 31–36, 38, 39–41, 67,
68–69, 72–73
and foreign exchange, 24–25
and private enterprise restrictions, 39–41
and property laws, 38
and reforms, 8, 9, 11–12, 25, 31–36, 38, 39–41,
67, 72–73
and self-employment, 24, 28–30, *37*
and the "Special Period," 24–25, 27
and state employment, 23, 31, 32, 33–34,
35–36, 39, 40
and subsidies from the USSR, 16, 20, 21, 23–24
and subsidies from Venezuela, 27–28, *29*, 68–69
and U.S. trade embargo, 20–21, 55, 60–61, 69, 71
Eisenhower, Dwight D., 20
embargo, trade, 20–21, 55, 60, 69, 71
See also economy, Cuban
embassy, American (in Cuba), 8, *70*
embassy, Cuban (in America), 8
entrepreneurship, 31, 34–35, *37*
restrictions on, 39–41
See also private enterprise
executive orders, 6, 20–21, 71

foreign exchange, 24–25
foreign relations. *See* U.S.-Cuba relations
Francis (Pope), 58

Freedom House, 50

García, Iván, 41
Gorbachev, Mikhail, 23–24
Gross, Alan P., 57–58, 59
Guevara, Che, *64*

Havana, Cuba, 12, 36, 48, *64*
American embassy in, 8, *70*
protests in, 43–44
health care, 27, 32
housing, 32, 38
human rights, 44, 45–48, 50–51
Human Rights Watch, 50

Internet access, 46–48, 60

Jewish community groups, 57

Kennedy, John F., 20
Khrushchev, Nikita S., *17*

Ladies in White (Damas de Blanco), *42*, 43–45, 46
Lenin, Vladimir, *19*
liberal democracy, 18, 19
See also capitalism
licenses, self-employment, 24, 28, *34*, 35, 40
See also private enterprise

means of production, 26, 31
media, 14
state control of, 11, 48, *49*, 50
mercenaries, 42, 45

nationalization, 6, 15

Obama, Barack, 46, 55–57, 58, 60, *68*
and normalization of U.S.-Cuba relations, 8–9,
11–12, *56*, 58–62
visit to Cuba of, *6*, 7, 8–9, *10*, 11–12
Obama, Michelle, 6, 7
oil, 16, 21, 24, 27–28, *29*, 68–69
Organization of American States (OAS), 56–57

political prisoners, 42, 44–45, 50, 59
Powell, Colin, 53
private enterprise, 26, 28–30, 31, 34–36, *37*
restrictions on, 39–41
and self-employment licenses, 24, 28, *34*, 35, 40

propaganda, 42, *49*, 50
property laws, 38

Radio Martí, 53–54
rations, 6, *33*
   and ration books, 23, *26*, 32, 41
remittances, 40–41, 55–56
research projects, 25, 41, 52, 63, 73
Rhodes, Ben, 58
Rodríguez, Bruno, 11
Ross, Joel, 67
Rowlandson, William, 67
Rubio, Marco, 62

Sánchez, Yoani, 46
self-employment, 24, 28–30, *34*, 41
   See also private enterprise
socialism, 18, 19, 20
   in Cuba, 22, 28–30, 31, 32–33, 62, 72–73
   See also communism
Soler, Berta, 46
Soviet Union. *See* Union of Soviet Socialist
   Republics (USSR)
"Special Period," 24–25, 27
state employment, 23, 31, 32, 33–34, 35–36, 39
   and salaries, 40
subsidies, 6, 21, 23–24, 27–28, *29*, 68–69

Taxi Rutero, 36
tourism, 25, 35, *37*, 40, 41, 60–61
travel, Cuban, 45–46
travel restrictions, U.S., 9, 11, *17*, 21, 55–56, 60–61
Trump, Donald, *70*, 71–72

undocumented immigrants, Cuban, 46
Union of Soviet Socialist Republics (USSR), 16–18,
   20, 21, 23–24
U.S. Agency for International Development
   (USAID), 57
U.S.-Cuba relations, 55–57
   and Fulgencio Batista, 12, 13–14
   and the Bay of Pigs invasion, 7, 20, *21*
   and George Bush, 53–55
   and economic sanctions, *17*, 21
   normalization of, 8–9, 11–12, *56*, 58–63, 67,
     72–73
   and trade embargo, 20–21, 55, 60, 69, 71
   and Donald Trump, 71–72
   and U.S. assassination attempts on Cuban lead-
     ers, 7–8

Venezuela, 27–28, *29*, 68–69
Vidal, Pavel, 69

Welles, Sumner, *13*

About the Author: John Ziff, a freelance writer and editor, has long been interested in Latin American history and culture. He lives outside Philadelphia.

Picture Credits: Library of Congress: 13, 15; used under license from Shutterstock, Inc.: 2, 29, 42; Cristiano Barni / Shutterstock.com: 66 (top); Bas Photo / Shutterstock.com: 54; Capture Light / Shutterstock.com: 34; Marco Crupi / Shutterstock.com: 64; Crush Rush / Shutterstock.com: 62; DayOwl / Shutterstock.com: 37; Fotos593 / Shutterstock.com: 26; GagliardiImages / Shutterstock.com: 38, 52; Jctabb / Shutterstock.com: 70; Gil. K / Shutterstock.com: 3; Kamira / Shutterstock.com: 61; Karis48 / Shutterstock.com: 10; Felix Lipov / Shutterstock.com: 19; Lulu and Isabelle / Shutterstock.com: 47; LunaseeStudios / Shutterstock.com: 21; Miami2you / Shutterstock.com: 66 (bottom); Neftali / Shutterstock.com: 14; Matyas Rehak / Shutterstock.com: 33; Kimberly Shavender / Shutterstock.com: 6, 9; Tupungato / Shutterstock.com: 22, 49; United Nations photo: 17, 30; official White House photo: 1, 56, 59, 68; Wikimedia Commons: 44.